She'll Find the Sky

A Collection of Poems

Christy Ann Martine

This book is dedicated to my wonderful husband John, and his two amazing children Ryan and Rachel, and to my children Sarah (The Girl on Fire), Quinn (The Scotsman), Heather (Scottish Heather), and Rachael (The Actress). Thank you for your love and support.

CONTENTS

Chapter One

Among the Trees

Wild Sky

She lost herself in the trees
among the ever-changing leaves.
She wept beneath the wild sky
as stars told stories of ancient times.
The flowers grew towards her light,
the river called her name at night.
She could not live an ordinary life
with the mysteries of the universe
hidden in her eyes.

Appreciation of Life

When your world moves too fast
and you lose yourself in the chaos,
introduce yourself
to each color of the sunset.
Reacquaint yourself
with the earth beneath your feet.
Thank the air that surrounds you
with every breath you take.
Find yourself
in the appreciation of life.

Sunrise Meditation

I am thankful for the brilliant sun
rising in the sky,
as the soft clouds drift
peacefully by.
I am grateful to be part
of this perfect moment in time,
on this masterpiece of a morning,
watching the world come alive.

Dance with the Waves

Dance with the waves,
move with the sea.
Let the rhythm of the water
set your soul free.

When the Forest Sings

The wind is rustling
the leaves of the trees
and the birds are singing along,
as I walk through the forest
listening to nature's song.

Journey of Life

You'll find my heart
in the deepest of oceans,
the highest of mountains,
the tallest of trees.
I'm in love with the sun,
each star in the sky,
this beautiful world
and the journey of life.

October Walk

The forest is calling,
the autumn leaves falling,
and summer is just out of reach.
Winter's still sleeping,
the sunlight is fleeting,
and the old trees are speaking to me.

Essence of Life

It's not enough to notice
the beautiful flowers
as you walk past them.
You need to reach
for their soft petals,
feel their essence,
remember what it is
to grow.

Wildflower

The sunlight dances in her hair
as she reaches for the sky.
She loves the rain, her spirit is free,
she is the most beautiful wildflower
that grows by the sea.

The Secrets of the Forest

When the soft winds blow
I can hear the trees whispering.
Their leaves rustling
as they share their thoughts
with the universe.
They talk about the sun, the sky,
the people that roam the earth.
They say we are all one.

Moonrise

The sunlight
is fading,
and the full moon
is waiting,
to rise above
the river birch trees.

Evening Soirée

The river rushes
to greet the trees
as they gather together
in the moonlight,
their leaves dressed
in slivers of silver.

Meet Me at Midnight

Meet me at midnight
in the forest of my dreams.
We'll make a fire
and count the stars
that shimmer above the trees.

Sleeping Moon

The moon has drifted
off to sleep,
a slumber so sublime,
as the last bit of darkness
escapes the morning sky.

Starry Night Dreams

I throw wishes
into the night,
and wait for the stars
to catch them.

Midnight Magic

Feel the soothing magic
of the midnight breeze
as the moon shines down
on the sleeping trees.

Music Maker

He walks through the forest,
listening to the trees.
He can hear their whispers
in the rustle of their leaves.
He lives upon the water
in a boat he made from dreams,
making music with his hands
while the river sings.
He's in love with nature,
he loves every living thing,
and the earth, she loves his spirit
for he lets his soul roam free.

Embrace the Storm

Dance beneath the stars
as you drink in the night,
let the thunder overtake you
as lightning fills the sky.
Feel the force of nature
penetrate your skin,
spin with the world
as the magic sinks in.

Sunday Afternoon

After a day of rain,
gray skies bend
to greet me on
the front porch.

Rain

I am the rain
gently patting
the rooftop,
the drop
sliding down
your window.
I glide past
the glow
of your lamp.
Clinging
to the warmth
of your fingertips
as they press
against the glass.
Losing grip,
I slip away.

Winter Waltz

The wind lifted me
up into the trees
where I danced
to the rhythm
of the evergreen,
swaying to the tune
of the northern breeze,
frozen in timeless melody.

December in Toronto

These city streets
are paved in gray,
on this rainy winter's day.
The houses lined against the sky,
I watch the people hurry by,
while bare trees speak
of simpler times.

Frosty Homecoming

The air is crisp as I trudge home
to see tiny palms on frozen glass.
Watching as the darkness falls
across the snowy lane.

Winter Forest

The forest has become
a winter's dream,
with snow-covered branches
and icy streams.
The cold winds blow
in from the north
while a nearby cabin
offers its warmth.

The Snow Angel

Downy flakes fall swiftly past
the glow of the streetlight.
A sprinkle of white flurries
cast against the dark of night.
The snow is crisp, the stars are bright,
I spread my wings and I take flight.
Wings fluttering as I fly,
up into the evening sky.

Chapter Two

Moments of Romance

Until the End of Time

I will love you
as long as the sun
burns in the sky,
as long as the moon
shines its light
into the dark night,
until the raging blue oceans
become calm and run dry.
I will love you until
the end of time.

If I Were the Sun

If I were the sun
and you were the sky,
I'd never set.
I'd hover above
the edge of the water,
waiting for you to shine
your stars on me,
so I could become
bigger than what I am.
I am brighter
when I'm with you.

Eternity

Sitting next to you
is like taking
a sip of eternity,
the sun, the stars,
the sky,
never tasted
so good.

Flourishing

Love is a soft rain,
gently falling
on my heart,
nourishing my soul
so it can grow.

Sunshower

Bathe me in sunlight
and pour your love on me,
so my heart can bloom.

Soulmates

I spent my days
waiting for you,
searching the crowds
for your face.
I stopped breathing
the moment you
recognized me,
as you captured my soul
with your gaze.

Late-Night Conversations

Your soft words
are sinking into my soul,
and I'm getting lost
in your story.

Opening My Heart to Him

I didn't know what love felt like
until he filled my heart
with pieces of himself.
I've never known such fullness,
an ocean of feelings overflowing
into the emptiest parts of me.

A Brighter Life with You

Have you noticed how the world
has changed since we met?
The moon has become fuller,
the stars have grown brighter,
and each day is filled
with endless amounts of hope.

Eternal Promise

I love you with a deeper love
than any human heart has ever known,
I love you with a soul
that has lived a thousand lifetimes,
always waiting to meet you again,
so I can promise to be yours forever.

Our Love Story

Love has written
the most beautiful story
on my soul,
and I will cherish these words,
each promise of forever,
every vow I have made to you.

Your Love Reminds Me of Summer

Cherry lips and raspberry wine,
jasmine flowers on climbing vines,
palm trees rustling in the sunshine,
wishing we could slow down time.

Dreams of a Full Moon

The roar of the ocean
holds secrets of
moonlight lovers.
Love rises with the tide,
it lives within the waves.

Star Gazing

She's a falling star,
burning in the night,
she's the shimmer on the water
in a river of moonlight.

Midnight Kisses

I met her by the sea,
beneath the silver moon,
where we shared midnight kisses,
made starry-eyed wishes,
and sunrise came too soon.

Cosmic Love

Promise me
we'll always be this free,
dancing for eternity,
underneath a galaxy of stars.

Burning for You in the Endless Summer

I am the fire that lights the stars,
and you my love are my universe.

The Horizon

My head is in the clouds.
Your feet are on the ground.
We meet at the horizon
in the place where the earth
touches the sky,
in the place where my dreams
become your reality.

Absolute Love

Shed your insecurities
and reveal yourself to me,
so I can see
each imperfection,
cherish every flaw,
get to know you
from the inside out,
for my love is raw.

First Glance

When I saw you
standing there
I finally knew
what happily ever after
looked like.

Extraordinary Moments

I haven't had
an ordinary day
since we met.
Each moment
spent with you
has been
nothing less
than extraordinary.

Moonlight Swim

She was so lovely
in the moonlight
that even the stars
wanted to know
her name.

Basking in the Glow of Love

You are the fire
that lights my soul
and keeps my heart
warm at night.

The Brightest Star

She shone so beautifully
in the darkness,
every star in the sky
envied her light.

Endless Possibilities

You told me
I could shape the world
with my mind.
That I could create
a whole new life.
You taught me how
to move the stars,
one at a time,
until new constellations
formed in the sky,
and thoughts
of endless possibilities
shone in my eyes.

Growing Together in Love

The day we met,
the seed was planted.
It was the perfect
season for love.

We were warmed
by the sun,
drank rain like wine,
and marveled
at the spring blossoms
we created.

Winter came,
the cold winds blew,
our branches snapped,
some of our dreams
were broken,
but we grew stronger
with each passing year.

Our hearts swell
beneath the earth,
we stand as one,
an ancient tree,
our roots
forever entangled
as we face
the sky together.

After the Long Winter

Open your heart to me
like the petals of a flower
greeting the morning sun,
bask in the warmth
of a new beginning,
learn to love again.

Rhythm of His Mind

I'm searching for the man
who can melt my frozen heart.
The one who will chip away
at my walls until they fall apart.
I look for him in dark places,
in the deepest corners of desire,
I'll find him in the morning sun,
he'll set my soul on fire.
He'll hold my heart next to his,
he'll read to me at night.
He'll dance with me
beneath the sheets
to the rhythm of his mind.
He'll fill me with his secrets,
bring me back to life;
he'll light me up
like the evening stars
so I'll burn throughout the night.

The Edge

His mind is filled
with beautiful things,
past revelations
and future sins.
He takes me to places
that I've never been,
to the edge of light
where darkness begins.

She Is Fire, He Is Ice

She is fire, he is ice.
One glimpse of her ignites
his stone-cold eyes.
The heat of her body
melts the frozen parts of his heart.
He walks through flames
just to feel her warmth.

Love Cocktail

He's the sweetest man
I've ever known.
He's heaven peppered
with a dash of hell.
I wish I knew how
to make love last forever,
I want to drink him in
for the rest of my life.

Forget the World

I want to feel our deep connection
so let your thoughts go,
leave your aching body
and touch me with your soul.

Lyrics of Your Life

I want to learn
the lyrics
of your life,
memorize each line,
so I can sing
the most beautiful
love song,
each note in tune
with our minds.

Young Love Ignites

Fire lived within his kiss,
he had a way of melting
every part of me.
The memory of his love
still burns in my heart,
the sweet taste of passion
lingers on my lips.

First Love's Kiss

I am fascinated
by the shape
of your lips
and how they fit
so perfectly
with the shape
of mine.

Melting into You

I wonder what
it would be like
to melt into
your sweet arms
and stay there
for eternity.

Soft Love

Wrap me in
the softest love
I have ever known,
show me that
I am not alone.

Sacred Places

I searched the darkest corners
of his soul
for the rarest type of beauty,
and accidentally found
pieces of myself
hidden in sacred places,
where the deepest secrets
of the heart reside.

Map to Your Heart

You told me where
you hid your heart,
drew me a map
to your secret hiding place.
I stumbled along
the narrow path,
listening for the sound
of your heartbeat.
The days were lonely,
and the nights were cold,
but I never stopped
searching for your warmth
before I finally found your love
in the place we call home.

Chapter Three

The Love of a Mother

A Mother's Love

A mother wraps her love
around the heart of her child,
keeping each beat steady
through the rhythm of life,
until wings take shape,
and it's time for the soul
to take flight.

Scottish Heather

She's like the sunlight
and sweet summer air,
wearing sprigs of white heather
in her strawberry hair.
Her heart is golden,
her eyes sea blue,
she holds seeds of wishes
that are starting to bloom.

—for my daughter Heather

The Actress

Her face so fair with long raven hair,
her eyes remind me of a bygone era.
She moves through the city
and the city moves through her.
Wearing a velvet dress
and *Parfum de Fleur.*
She's the star of her own story
and you'll want to watch the show,
a woman from another time,
a time so long ago.

—for my daughter Rachael

The Scotsman

He's fearless and loyal
with fiery hair,
his long-ago home
the Island of Barra.
He has the blood of a Viking
and a motto so fierce,
the heart of a highlander
and a warrior spirit.

—*for my son Quinn*

The Spark of Adoration

Her red hair burns
like the rays of the sun,
I see her and I am lit,
for she is beautiful
beyond compare,
the girl with blue eyes
and fire for hair.

—for my daughter Sarah

The Girl on Fire

The raven-haired boy
swooped down to admire
the girl on fire.
He reached for her
as she danced in the flames,
singeing his wings on desire.
She gave him her hand
and they flew to new heights,
where she burned
as bright as the stars.
And when their love ignites
on warm summer nights,
their glow can be seen from afar.

—for Sarah and her love, Adam

The Heart of a Mother

The soft rains that fall
before rainbows appear,
the flowers that burst
with color in spring,
cannot compare
to the beauty
that blooms within
the heart of a mother.

Chapter Four

When the Sky Falls

The Day My Love Left Me

The moon split in half
and the stars crumbled,
falling like fireworks into the sea.
I watched my world fall apart
the day my love left me.

Searching for Love

He lights a single candle
and sails into the night,
a flicker of hope upon the water
in the lonely sea of life.

Sitting by the Shore Missing You

My heart sinks
as I watch the sun
slip into the sea.
Another day
lost in the waves
without my love
here with me.

Burning Embers

I was drawn to your flame,
inspired by your fire,
you set my heart ablaze
as I burned with desire.

But the rain was heavy
and the wind was strong,
passion can't burn
once the heat is gone.

On the coldest nights
I'll look for your glow
among the burning embers
of your fiery soul.

I'll sift through the ashes
in search of the spark
that ignited my mind
and lit up my heart.

Frozen Heart

I chipped away
at your cold exterior,
dodging shards of ice
until you were
no longer hard.
But even though
I cracked the surface,
your heart
would not melt.

When We Say Goodbye

Hold me through the fire
as the stars are falling,
and our love turns to ashes
beneath the empty sky.

Worth Keeping

Hold on to your heart
when love falls apart,
and you feel like nothing
you have is worth keeping.

Broken Memories

Hearts heal
but never forget
how it feels
to be broken.

Scraps of Love

We hold on to our broken dreams,
while searching for scraps of love
in a pile of distant memories.

Missing Her

Her dust is nestled
between the sheets
where she used to
read herself to sleep.
Now I lie in bed
with her books,
grieving the scent
of her pillow.

Faded Dreams

I'll gather up our memories
and put them in a box,
so I can pull them out on rainy days,
and the days we barely talk.
They'll remind me of who we were
before the ticking of the clock
turned our love into faded dreams.
I'll feel what we forgot.

Haunted

When love dies
it becomes
a lonely ghost,
haunting our hearts
forever.

Fading Light

Even the sky
must learn
to say goodbye
to the stars.

Chapter Five

Whimsical Words

Jar of Dreams

If only I could catch my dreams
and keep them in a jar.
I'd watch them dance like fireflies,
flickering like stars.
They would grow and I'd let them go
to see how far they'd fly,
lighting up the pitch-black night
as they soar throughout the sky.

The Wanderers of Life

The wanderers of life
are made of earth and sky.
They see the universe
with stars in their eyes.

Wild, Wicked and Free

I was made to be wild,
wicked and free,
to carve out my own
crazy destiny,
to find a place
in this world
where I can be
the most authentic
version of me.

The Blue Sky Is Calling

The blue sky is calling to me,
asking me to join the clouds.
Rising above the earth,
I will soar to new heights,
and find freedom in the wind.

My Own Piece of Sky

If only I could fly,
I'd find a piece of sky
to call home.

The Girl on Fire at Burning Man

She is lighting up
the desert sky
with a fire that will burn
for the rest of her life.

Dancing in the Desert with the Girl on Fire

She dances in the desert rain,
her hair falling like flames,
and the crowd burns with desire,
as they watch this beautiful fire.

Sarah's Song

She dances with fire
to the song of the stars,
her name is written
in the flames.

Immortal

We are shining like stars,
wishing we would never fall,
wanting to burn forever.

Sunset Wishes

Let's watch the stars
fill the night with magic.

Stars of Hope

The stars are filled with wishes,
made on long, lonely nights.

Infinite Love

My heart belongs
to the universe,
I've learned to love
with my soul.

The Magic in Me

I see the magic in everything,
and hope the world
can see the magic in me.

Forgotten Dreams

I lost my dreams in the sea,
but the waves brought
them back to me.

Whimsical Girl

She had a mischievous smile,
curious heart, and an affinity
for running wild.

Songs of the Sky

My dreams were born with wings,
and all my soul ever sings
are songs of the sky.

Chapter Six

Sparks of Inspiration

Hopes of a Writer

I want someone to read these words
and understand me for just one second
so I'm not alone with my thoughts.

Creative Flow

Words swim inside my head
as I drift into a lyrical sea.
Emotions flow in rhythmic waves
as diluted thoughts flood the page.
Paper drenched in melodic verse,
passion surges and I'm submerged,
drowning in inspiration
as ink drips from my pen.

The Blaze

Set fire to my pen.
Ignite my words
until they're seared
into your memory.
When emotions smolder
and paper turns to ash,
sift remnants for lyrics,
pull verse from remains,
until inspiration sparks
and my pen is lit again.

The Poem That Lives Within

If only you could see the words
buried beneath my skin,
you'd see who I was born to be,
the poem that lives within.

Tapestry of Words

Let me wrap my words around you
so you know you're not alone.
Give me your loose threads
so I can weave them into a poem.

Finding Inspiration in the Morning Sky

I want to fill the sky with words
so poems rain down on me,
washing away my inhibitions,
leaving me with nothing but inspiration.

Empty Evenings

Let me fill you with my words
so you'll feel less empty tonight.

How Would You Paint Me?

If you were an artist
how would you paint me?
With deep solid strokes
or your brush sweeping softly?

Would you paint me by number,
quickly fill in the lines
or sketch me first,
taking your time?

Would you use vibrant colors
or plain shades of gray?
Would you change me
in any way?

Would you hang me up proudly
and gaze at me often,
or tuck me away
until I'm forgotten?

The Dancer

I met an artist,
now my days are painted
in lavender, every hour
a different hue.

I dream in watercolor,
dance in blurred tones,
with each stroke I glide,
moved by inspiration.

I am his vision, his dancer,
his impression of beauty,
this canvas my stage
as I perform for you.

Uninhibited

I want to lose myself in the music,
give my soul to art,
forget that I have a name,
and become the kind of beautiful
that is only found in the heart.

Restless Words

When there are
too many words
inside of my head
I cannot sleep.
They rattle around
making all sorts of noise
until I pluck them out
of my mind
and put them on paper.
My voice
refuses to be silenced
by a downy pillow.

Always Searching

I see you flipping
through the pages of my life.
You think you know me
by the way I've written my story.
You read sorrowful verses
penned on ink smudged pages,
and no matter how hopeless
the words seem, you are always hoping.
You hope to be renewed.
I have poured my essence onto paper
so you can feel alive through my eyes,
so you can feel how wonderful
this strange world can be,
when you choose to live,
to really live,
among the trees, and the animals,
and in the hearts of the people
who roam the city streets.
We are always needing,
always searching,
for something,
for anything
that makes us feel alive.

You're Not Alone

I'm just another writer,
who speaks to you in poems,
trying to help you find your way
through life's bitter storms.
I'll help you fight the battle,
you'll never be alone,
and when you're lost
I'll be the voice
leading you back home.
I can be your mother,
your sister or your friend.
I'll be the words
you need to hear,
my love will never end.

Chapter Seven

The Dark Years

Warning:
This chapter contains dark subject matter,
including abuse, neglect, and depression.

Luminosity

Generational abuse
is not my spiritual birthright,
I was born into darkness,
but I am made of light.

Mother

Your smile is as beautiful
as your long, golden hair,
but looks can be deceiving
in the dragon's lair.

When you open your mouth,
fire pours out,
scorching my soul,
burning holes in my heart.

These scars do not fade,
they do not heal with time,
but I look for the clearing
in the dark sky.

When the smoke clears
and these tears finally dry,
I will see what love looks like
for the first time.

Stay

All I've ever wanted
is to fill
these empty spaces
in my heart
with the type of love
that never leaves.

Yearning for Her Love

Your love drips
through the cracks
of my broken heart.
Some of us
are never meant
to be full.

Empty

Loneliness is emptiness
begging to be filled.

Escape from Reality

Only the broken know
what it's like to live inside
of their imagination.
Creating worlds to dream in,
we are artists of the mind.
Our true gift is survival.

Trapped

She was too young
to be left behind.
Now she searches for herself
in between the lines,
trapped in the pages
of another time.
The story of a girl
who learned to survive.

Angel of the Highway

Trapped behind steel
with your hands on the wheel,
your words slurred,
your vision blurred,
and even though we lived,
there were parts of me that died,
while I begged for God to help me
on all those drunken nights.

Your Words Couldn't Break Me

You tried so hard
to shatter my spirit,
but a soul full of love
can never be broken.

Hollow

I would fill you with my love
if you weren't so hollow,
give you the depths of my soul
if you weren't so shallow.

The Aching Heart

I have a deep hole
inside my heart
where your love should be.
I need you to feel
so this wound can heal.
This emptiness
is killing me.

Unforgivable

I want to forgive you,
and I'd love to forget,
if only you were capable
of genuine regret.

Threads of Hope

Pain is carved into my heart,
wrapped in threads of hope
to keep it from falling apart.
My love is covered with scars.

Father

I waited by the window,
red ribbons in my hair,
for a man who never came,
a father never there.
He said that he was coming,
and so I waited there,
until morning turned to night,
red ribbons in my hair.

The Yearly Visit

I was invisible to you,
a transparent figure
sitting by your feet,
watching you read
the newspaper.
And I dreamed
that one day
you would look at me
the way you looked
at those words,
that you would be
interested in my story.

Hidden

She hid in the shadows
because she didn't believe
she was worthy of light.

Hunted

The sky is dark again today,
and this grayness surrounds me
like a pack of wolves
waiting to devour.

Find Me When I Am Lost

My life is a revolving door
between fantasy and reality.
I get lost inside of my nightmares
only to be found in my dreams.

Heartless

I made the mistake
of giving my heart
to someone who
didn't have one.

Nothing but His Darkness

He doesn't see the beauty
in the clear blue sky above.
He never took the time
to stop and feel my love.
He's like a breath of poison,
lingering in my lungs.
He gives me
nothing but his darkness,
but wants me to be his sun.

Insatiable

I sacrificed my heart,
fed it to you piece by piece.
But it didn't satisfy
your insatiable need
to hurt and devour;
you wanted all of the power.
So I offered up my soul,
hoping to appease
your all-consuming greed,
and you watched me struggle,
suffer and bleed,
before taking another
bite of me.

The Girl I Used to Be

He stripped away my self-worth,
layer by layer,
until there was nothing left
of my personality.
Yet I never forgot about
the girl I used to be.
She lived inside my caged soul,
waiting for the day
I would set her free.
Casting her light
into my dark mind,
hoping that I would see,
flashes of a better life,
glimpses of possibility.
I was never alone
because she believed in me.

Wasted Years

Nothing I did
was ever good enough.
All that love I gave to you
I should have given to myself.

Waiting for the Storm

She's in the clouds,
heavy and dark,
waiting to fall like rain.

When the Past Lingers

The night sinks into my bones.
The wind blows through me.
As I stand in the graveyard
of our memories,
I'm haunted by a ghost
that only I can see.

Followed

No matter where I go
or who I'm with,
loneliness always finds me.

Digging

You buried me
so deep in lies
it's taken years
to dig myself out.

Waiting for Love

I want to live
in a world
where love falls
from the sky like rain,
washing the pain
of the past away.

Tears of the Sun

The sun hid her face in the clouds,
she didn't want the world to see her cry.
Her teardrops burned holes in the horizon,
she lost her desire to shine.

Holding It Together Through the Storm

She held up
the sky,
while the pain
poured down
like rain.

The Darkest Memories

I left my memories behind
in search of freedom,
but they still follow me
as I walk towards the future.
Dark thoughts
of a different life,
where dreams
spend their days in a cage,
and love is nothing but pain.

No Escape from Pain

Running through the trees
in her dreams,
she trips over jagged roots,
and becomes tangled in
the overgrown brush.

The birds in the sky
warn her
that her memories
are close behind.

Twisted branches
reach for her,
the earth rises up
to swallow her,
as pain echoes
through the woods,
lingering in the leaves.

The Nightmares That Haunt Me

These nightmares wrap their evil hands
around my soul at night,
they try to pull me deep within
a world that's ruled by fright.
These dark thoughts may follow me
but they'll never win the fight.
I'll escape the looming shadows
with the help of dawn's first light.

Cold Rain

The colors of the rainbow
bleed onto the street,
dripping down the cracks,
sticking to my feet.
Nothing but the cold rain
can wash these stains away,
and return the colors
to the sky
on a day this gray.

I Need to Let Go

My mind is dark
and filled with pain,
like the dark sky
before the rain,
I need to let go.

Lonely World

Living on a planet filled with people,
it is a tragedy that any one of us
could ever feel this alone.

Within Reach

Surrounded by darkness,
I couldn't see,
that hope was
reaching out to me.

Carry Me

On those rainy days
when the sky grows dark,
I can feel the storm
brewing inside of me.
Clouding my thoughts.
Weighing down my heart.
I find solace in the gray clouds
that move easily through the sky.
They will carry me to the clearing
where rays of sunlight still shine.

I'll Be the One

Gray skies follow me,
through the crowds,
to other towns.
Heavy clouds
weigh me down.
But I'm going
to be the one
that rises up
and finds the sun.

Hold On

Everything beautiful
fades into darkness
if we don't hold on
to the light.

Chapter Eight

Reaching for the Light

She'll Find the Sky

You can't keep her in a cage,
clip her wings, tell her lies,
say that fragile birds
were never meant to fly.
Watch her live behind
a rusted door, latched tight,
her spirit slipping away
so you can keep her in sight.
Beautiful creatures
cannot be confined.
Her wings will grow,
she'll find the sky.

I Will Show You

I won't let pain
turn my heart
into something ugly.
I will show you
that surviving
can be beautiful.

Flower in the Desert

Like a flower in the desert
I had to grow in the cruelest weather,
holding on to every drop of rain
just to stay alive.
But it's not enough to survive,
I want to bloom beneath the blazing sun,
and show you all of the colors
that live inside of me.
I want you to see what I can become.

The Transformation

This is the chapter of my story
where I trade a lifetime of fear
for a lifetime of freedom
by learning how to fight.
It's the part where I transform
from victim to hero
on every page that I write
for the rest of my life.

Edge of Darkness

I've been to the edge of darkness
in a world of endless nights.
I've seen what forever looks like
in the darkest place of life,
and I've come back to tell you
that living is worth the fight.
We were born to feel
the sun on our skin,
our souls are made of light.

And Still You Shine

You have survived
the darkest of times
and still you shine.
You are a star
that never dies,
you have become
the hope in the night.

The Courage Within

Just when I thought
I'd run out of courage,
I found an endless
well of bravery
in the depths of my soul.

My Rising Sun

The darkness is heavy
but I am strong,
and courage has become
my rising sun.
Carrying me through the night,
helping me to go on,
leading me to the light
of the breaking dawn.

The Day I Was Rescued

Courage became my hero,
inner strength my miracle,
I was rescued by self-love.

What She Needs to Hear

Instead of asking her
why she didn't leave
her abuser sooner,
tell her you are proud of her
for leaving when she could.

Hopeful Sky

The sky is filled
with hope tonight,
each star a promise
of a better life.

New Beginnings

I will bury my tears
beneath the ground
and wait for new life
to grow.

Illumination

I am terribly broken
and know darkness well,
but the light inside of me
has a story to tell.

The Fire Inside

The stars are burning out
and it's never been this dark,
but nothing can destroy
the fire inside my heart.

Inferno

I want to set my life on fire,
watch my pain go up in flames,
burn as hot as an inferno,
I'm going to torch these chains.

The Long Journey

I have walked on broken dreams
with sorrow on my back.
I have stumbled as I carried
the weight of my past.
The path I took was painful,
and the journey, it was slow,
until at last I finally learned
how to let go.

Metamorphosis

There is so much beauty
in letting go of pain,
watching scars
turn into butterflies,
before they fly away.

Victorious

I am everything
you didn't give to me.
I am love, I am strength,
I am victory.

Burning Star

I won't let the darkness
hide my inner light,
I will burn with the brightest
stars in the night.

A Brighter Day Awaits

Keep searching for the colors
when everything turns gray.
Even in your darkest moments
a brighter day awaits.

Flowering Season

The flowers growing
inside of my heart
are finally ready
to bloom.

Everyday Hero

You don't have to be brave,
you just have to keep trying.
You don't have to be strong,
you just have to keep going.
Maybe your superpower
is refusing to give up,
even on your weakest days
when you feel you're not enough.

Survivors Anthem

Wounded hearts beat the loudest.

Her Story

She dipped her wings in ink,
to cover up her scars,
and wrote her story in the sky,
her words lit up like stars.

Butterfly Girl

You carry your pain
with such grace and beauty,
hiding your scars
beneath the wings
of a butterfly.

Come Home to Me

Beautiful girl,
lost in the world,
how brave you are
to have made it this far.

Traveling girl,
I know who you are,
we share the same pain,
we wear the same scars.

Crying girl,
hang on to me,
I will show you the hope,
all the hope that I've seen.

Runaway girl,
come home to me,
follow the stars
you see in your dreams.

Hope in the Dark

I wish I could take
the colors from a rainbow
and place them into your heart,
so you would remember
what beautiful feels like,
and know there is hope in the dark.

Love Is Everywhere

When your world grows dark
and your soul feels heavy,
rise up to meet the sky,
spend the night with infinity.
Let the universe wrap
its arms around you
as you draw courage from the stars.
Rest your weary head on hope,
and know that you are loved,
for love is everywhere.

There Will Always Be Light

When the gray clouds
roll into your life,
and your tears fall like rain
long into the night,
remember the sun
continues to shine.
Above the darkness
there will always be light.

Chapter Nine

Heaven's Whispers

She's in the Sun

She's in the sun, the wind, the rain,
she's in the air you breathe
with every breath you take.
She sings a song of hope and cheer,
there's no more pain, no more fear.
You'll see her in the clouds above,
hear her whisper words of love,
you'll be together before long,
until then listen for her song.

Little Dove

Little dove I love you so,
but I know you had to go.
So spread your wings
and fly my love,
soar above the world my dove.
Paint the sky in indigo,
let your graceful colors flow,
and I'll search the sky
for your rainbow.

Heaven's Cradle

Up above, a small child swings,
blanketed by angels' wings.
When she rocks all heaven sings,
a lullaby of love.

Don't Cry for Me

Don't cry for me, I'm not gone.
My soul is at rest, my heart lives on.
Light a candle for me to see,
and hold on to my memory,
but save your tears for I'm still here,
by your side, through the years.

Golden Shore

You will find me in heaven,
singing with the angels,
in a field of wildflowers
with sunlight in my hair.
Our memories are flowing,
like fallen leaves in the river,
and I'll wait for you forever
on this endless golden shore.

Your Love Lives Forever

Even though death
has torn us apart,
your love lives forever
inside of my heart.

Forever Free

There's an empty space
where you used to lay,
and a pain in my heart
that won't go away.
I couldn't have asked
for a better friend.
You were my
faithful companion
until the end.
Now you're
roaming endless fields,
forever free to run.
Listening to
the song of the wind
beneath the golden sun.
Meet me at the rainbow,
when the time is right.
Run into my arms again,
walk with me into the light.

Chapter Ten

Little Life Sayings

Happiness lives inside
of the smallest moments.

—*look for these joyous moments each day*

A mind filled
with gratitude
leads to a heart
full of happiness.

—*experience the joy of appreciation*

Let kindness flow
like a hopeful river,
filling this barren world
with love.

—have an ever-flowing heart

Create a safe place
within yourself
that no one will ever find,
somewhere the madness
of this world
can never touch.

—*build an inner sanctuary*

When life becomes so loud
that I can no longer
hear my own thoughts,
I need to turn down the volume
and tune into my soul,
so I can remember who I am
and where I am going.

*—your inner voice is always speaking to you,
  but you need to listen*

If only we could
believe in ourselves
the way God
believes in us,
we could
accomplish anything.

—use the unique gifts you've been given

Fill your glass with kindness
and offer a drink
to everyone you meet.

—pour love from your soul

We should all find
a quiet place,
a peaceful space,
to bury the chaos
and rest for a while.

—*make time for restful moments*
of solitude

When you feel lost,
listen to your soul.
It will tell you
where to go.

—*be intuitive*

A dream that seems out of reach
is often only a few steps
outside of your comfort zone.

—*you're closer than you think*

Every climb to the top
begins with looking up
and believing it's possible.

—look up and believe

Begin each day
with appreciation,
because this life
you're living
is your own creation.

—*create days filled with moments of joy*

A peaceful mind
leaves the past behind,
and learns to experience
each moment in time
as a spectacular gift
that's been given.

—give yourself the gift of letting go

If you've been through trauma
you don't need more drama,
so surround yourself with those
who bring you peace.

—*you have the power to create*
a calm and peaceful life

You deserve to be loved
by someone who knows
that love should never hurt.

— *genuine love is a gentle love*

Protect your heart
from anyone
who doesn't see
the value of your love.

—you are valuable, keep your heart safe

I became my own hero
the day I learned to say no.

—*you are worthy of self-protection*

If only we spent more time
singing love songs to ourselves.

—*deeply love and cherish yourself*

You can't receive the gifts
the present moment is offering
if you are living in the past.

—you don't have to hold on to the pain
forever, let go

Thank you for being the person
who asks what my tears mean,
rather than just wiping them away.

—*be the one who truly listens*

There are many types
of beautiful in this world
and you are one of them.

—*you have always been*
  an exquisite beauty

I hope life
gives you wings,
and you have
the courage
to use them.

—*may you find the sky*

About the Author

Christy Ann Martine lives in Ontario, Canada and is married to American poet and author John Mark Green. She is the mother of four adult children and two adult stepchildren. Christy is an abuse survivor who has struggled with anxiety and depression since early childhood.

She began sharing her poems online in 2014. Since then, they have been widely shared on social media and in online magazines such as *Good Housekeeping, Woman's Day, Country Living, Parade, and Cosmopolitan.*

Celebrities around the world have shared her poetry on their social media accounts, including Julian Lennon, Misha Collins, The Jacksons, Mena Suvari, *Good Bones* star Mina Starsiak Hawk, actress Amyra Sastur, and TV personality Matt Johnson.

Since opening her Etsy poetry shop in 2014 she has sold nearly five thousand poems to date. Her poetry has been transformed into inspiring choral songs and have been published in several books, including Gill Education's *Over the Moon: The Wild Explorers*, *O'Words Anthology*, *Gamemaster* from the Biodome Chronicles book series, and *Latitudes Inspirations* nature photography book.

Her poem "She'll Find the Sky" was read in Scottish Parliament as the introduction to a Domestic Abuse Bill debate in September 2017, and the gender-neutral version of the poem was included in a short film on the theme of domestic violence titled *Joan's Song*.

Christy Ann Martine's greatest hope in life is for her poetry to offer hope, encouragement, and comfort to her readers.

Acknowledgments

Thank you to the love of my life, John, for the tremendous amount of love and support you have given me since we met. Your belief in me as a writer is the reason that I was able to overcome my insecurities and finish this book. You are a wonderful husband and I adore you.

Thank you to Sarah, Quinn, Heather, and Rachael for being a source of inspiration and for your warmth, love, and encouragement. You are the stars that light up my sky, each one of you shining in your own unique way. The love I have for you is never-ending.

Rachel, thank you so much for your encouragement. I am so grateful for your love and positivity. You are a beautiful light in this world, and my heart is filled with love for you.

Ryan, you are a quiet hero, courageous and inspiring. I appreciate your warmth and kindness. I love you.

Adam, Will, and Simon, thank you so much for your love and words of encouragement. I love you all. You are strong, optimistic men destined for great success, and your kind words make me believe that I too will succeed.

And lots of love to my beautiful ladies, Jess, Phaon (Traveling Girl), and Cheyanne.

Thank you to my social media followers for sharing my poems, taking the time to offer words of encouragement, and letting me know that my writing has made a positive difference in your life. You have filled my heart and soul with your love.

To my Etsy customers, thank you for supporting my creative writing efforts by purchasing my poems. You have made my dreams of becoming a full-time writer a reality. You have shared your life stories with me and showered me with words of kindness. I appreciate your love and support with all my heart.

Christy's hand-typed poems are available for purchase in her Etsy shop: etsy.com/ca/shop/ChristyAnnMartine

For business inquiries and licensing permissions contact: christyannmartine@gmail.com

Follow Christy Ann Martine on social media:

Instagram: @christy_ann_martine

Facebook: @christyannmartine

Pinterest: @christyamartine

Printed in Great Britain
by Amazon

25120545R00148